LITTLE
LOST
BEE

By Joan Kapral

Illustrations by Richard Mlodock

 CHILDRENS PRESS, CHICAGO

Library of Congress Cataloging in Publication Data

Kapral, Joan.
   Little lost bee.

   SUMMARY: From two spiders to nine fireflies, the
other animals help one lost bee find his way home to
his ten brothers.
   [1.   Stories in rhyme.   2.   Animals—Stories.
3.   Counting books]   I.   Mlodock, Richard, illus.
II.   Title.
PZ8.3.K126Li   398.8 [E]   72-1466
ISBN 0-516-03536-3

Library of Congress Catalog Card Number: 72-1466

1 2 3 4 5 6 7 8 9 10 11 12 13 14 15 16 17 18 19 20 21 22 23 24 25 R 75 74 73 72

LITTLE LOST BEE

One little bee
Left all alone
Flew around
Looking for home.

Two tiny spiders
Spinning webs
Said to the bee,
"It's straight ahead."

Three flowers waving
In the air
Nodded to the bee,
"Over there."

Four berries hid
The nest from sight.
The bee flew by
Filled with fright.

Five ants told him,
"Go back. It's dark.
You passed your home
Back in the park."

Six tears dropped
From the bee's brown eyes.
He stopped his search
And sat and cried.

17

Seven frogs croaked,
"The bee is sad.
Let's help him home.
We'll leave our pad."

Eight bluebirds sang,
"This way. This way.
Your home is near.
We'll lead the way."

Nine fireflies flew
Around the nest.
They lit his home.
Now he could rest.

Ten bees glad
To see each other
Promised never
To leave one another.

1
ONE

2
TWO

3
THREE

4
FOUR

5
FIVE

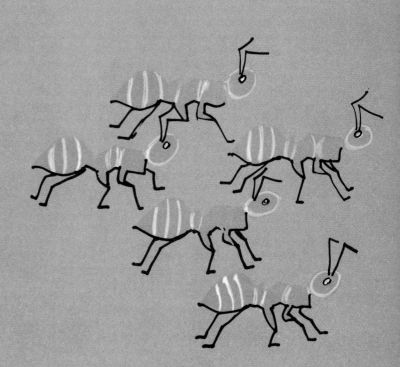

27

6
SIX

7
SEVEN

8
EIGHT

9
NINE

10
TEN

About the Author: A student at Southern Connecticut State College in New Haven, Connecticut, Joan Kapral wrote *Little Lost Bee* as an alternative to taking the final exam in a childrens' literature course. Encouraged by her professor, she decided to submit the manuscript to a publisher. Although she doesn't enjoy the tedious, yet necessary, details involved in writing, she loves her feeling of accomplishment when a work is completed. She writes only when an idea hits her and she is in the mood to write. Joan Kapral reads as much as she can, has acquired an interest in ceramics, does some crocheting, and sews most of her clothes.

About the Artist: Mr. Mlodock is a graduate of the Art Institute of Chicago. Painting, his family and outdoor living are the most important things in his life, but he is a communications buff, as well. From videotape through photography, one of his greatest challenges is to create something out of nothing. He lives with his family in suburban Deerfield, Illinois.